D0187900

Irish Blessings

Irish Blessings

Compiled with an Introduction
by
Ashley Shannon

RUNNING PRESS
PHILADELPHIA • LONDON

Library of Congress Cataloging-in-Publication Number
98-066648
ISBN 0-7624-0450-7

This book may be ordered by mail from the publisher.
Please include $1.00 for postage and handling.
But try your bookstore first!

Running Press Book Publishers
125 South Twenty-second Street
Philadelphia, Pennsylvania 19103-4399

Log onto www. Special Favors. com to order Running Press®
Miniature Editions™ with your own custom-made covers!
Visit us on the web!
www.runningpress.com

Contents

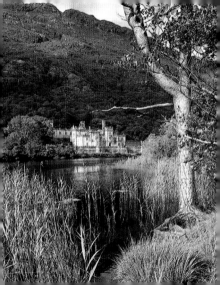

Introduction

The Irish have always been a spiritual people—even before St. Patrick arrived to convert them to Christianity in the fifth century. Warmth and kindness, generosity and goodwill invigorate the spiritual heritage of Ireland, and all of these traits are preserved in the traditional blessings featured in this book, which have been passed down from generation to generation among Irish families and spread throughout the world by Irish missionaries and emigrants.

The Irish landscape is itself a blessing. From the rolling fields of Munster to the gentle hills of Killarney, from the spectacular coastal scenery of the Dingle Peninsula to the desolate western beauty of Connemara, Ireland deserves its reputation as one of the loveliest of countries. It's said that 40 shades of green are found among the fields and vales of Ireland and any visitor can see why. Even on the greyest of days, Ireland's greens seem to glow with a life of their own: the soft moss growing on crumbling stone walls, the verdant lawns surrounding the country estates, the dark ivy creeping on cottages—all of these are variations on a lush theme which weaves itself into a symphony of color.

The intensity of the landscape of the Emerald Isle has conquered the hearts of people around the world, even those who are "Irish" only on St. Patrick's Day. Ireland holds power over the imagination like no other land, offering to each person an opportunity to discover an individual sense of beauty. Whether one prefers the austere beauty of a ruined monastery buried deep in the Tipperary countryside or the bustle and Georgian splendor of Dublin's streets, Ireland has as many personalities as it does shades of green.

This book captures the beauty of the island in all its moods. The blessings and poems express the good humor and generous hospitality that are essential parts of the Irish character—not to mention the poetic turn of phrase or occasional irreverent witticism so distinctive to Irish writing. The accompanying pictures evoke the landscape where these traits were forged. Together with the invocation for "soft rain and easy roads" in the best-known of Irish blessings, or W. B. Yeats's homage to the call of his lake isle while standing on the "pavements grey," they capture the eternal essence of the holy land of Ireland.

Blessings
from the
Land of Eire

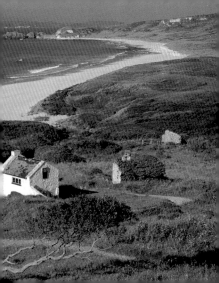

I am of Ireland
And of the holy land of Ireland
Good sir I pray of ye
For saintly charity
Come dance with me
In Ireland.

Anonymous
14th-century Irish poet

May the Irish Hills caress you.

May her lakes and rivers
bless you.

May the luck of the Irish
enfold you.

May the blessings of Saint
Patrick behold you.

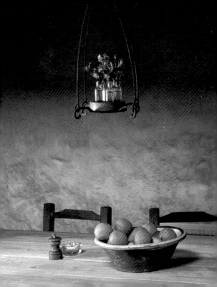

BLESSINGS FROM THE LAND OF EIRE

An old Irish recipe
for longevity:

✠ ✠ ✠

Leave the table hungry.

Leave the bed sleepy.

Leave the table thirsty.

✠

Ireland, it's the one place
on earth

That heaven has kissed

With melody, mirth,

And meadow and mist.

May your heart be warm and
      happy
With the lilt of Irish laughter
Every day in every way
And forever and ever after.

When Erin first rose from
    the dark swelling flood

God bless'd the Emerald Isle,
    and saw it was good;

The em'rald of Europe,
    it sparked and shone—

In the ring of the world,
    the most precious stone.

William Drennan
Irish poet (1754–1820)

Now sweetly lies old
Ireland,

Emerald green beyond
the foam,

Awakening sweet
memories,

Calling the heart back
home.

Eire

Where the wind has a sound
like a sweet song,

And anyone can hum it,

And the heather grows upon
the hills

And shamrocks not far
from it.

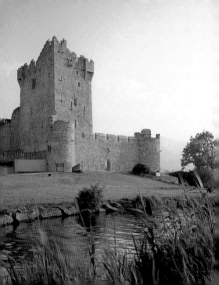

May the luck of the Irish be
always at hand,

And good friends always
near you.

May each and every coming
day

Bring some special joy to
cheer you.

BLESSINGS FROM THE LAND OF EIRE

When Irish eyes are smiling,
Sure it's like a morning spring.
In the lilt of Irish laughter
You can hear the angels sing.
When Irish hearts are happy,
All the world seems bright and
gay.
And when Irish eyes are smiling,
They'll steal your heart away!

Traditional Irish Folk Song

St. Patrick's
Breast plate

Christ be with me,

Christ be within me,

Christ behind me,
     Christ before me,

Christ beside me,
     Christ to win me,

Christ to comfort me,
     Christ above me,

Christ in quiet,
Christ in danger

Christ in hearts
of all that love me

Christ in mouth of friend
and stranger.

St. Patrick
5th-century Irish cleric

A fruitful clime is Eire's,
    through valley, meadow,
    plain,
And in the fair land of Eire, O!
The very 'bread of life' is in
    the yellow grain
On the fair Hills of Eire, O!

28

Far dearer to me than the
    tones music yields,

Is the lowing of the kine and
    the calves in her fields

And the sunlight that shone
    long ago on the shields

Of the Gaels, on the fair hills
    of Eire, O!

James Clarence Mangan
Irish poet (1803–1849)

29

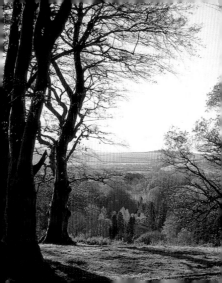

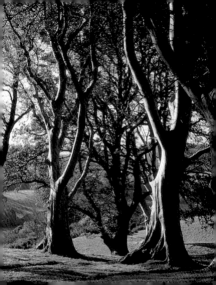

Hills as green as emeralds
    Cover the countryside,

Lakes as blue as sapphires
    Are Ireland's special pride,

And rivers that shine like silver
    Make Ireland look so fair—

But the friendliness of her people
    Is the richest treasure
    there.

The pillar towers of Ireland,
>how wondrously they stand
By the lakes and rushing rivers
>through the valleys
>of our land
In mystic file, through the isle,
>they lift their heads sublime,
These gray old pillar temples,
>these conquerors of time!

Denis McCarthy
Irish poet (1817–1882)

Were you ever in Tipperary, where
    the fields are so sunny and green,
And the heath-brown Slieve-bloom
    and the Galtees look down with
    so proud a mien?
'Tis there you would see more beauty
    than is on all Irish ground—
God bless you, my sweet Tipperary,
    for where could your match be
    found?

Mary Kelly
Irish poet (1825–1910)

May the saints protect ye—
    An' sorrow neglect ye,
An' bad luck to the one
    That doesn't respect ye!
T' all that belong to ye,
    An long life t' yer honor—
That's the end of my song
    t' ye!

May your thoughts be as glad
as the shamrocks.

May your heart be as light as a
song.

May each day bring you bright
happy hours,

That stay with you all year long.

For each petal on the
   shamrock
This brings a wish your *way*—
Good health, good luck, *and*
   happiness
For today and every day.

May Ireland's voice
be ever heard,

Amid the world's
applause!

And never be her
flag-staff stirred

But in an honest cause!

Thomas Davis
Irish poet (1814–1845)

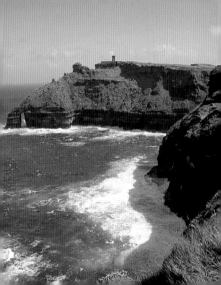

May your blessings
outnumber
The Shamrocks
that grow,
And may trouble
avoid you
Wherever you go.

When the first light of sun—
   Bless you.

When the long day is done—
   Bless you.

In your smiles and your tears—
   Bless you.

Through each day of your years—
   Bless you.

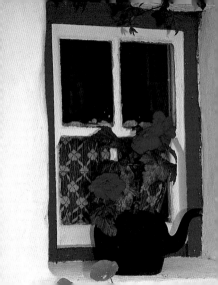

May you always have these
blessings . . .
A soft breeze when summer
comes,
A warm fireside in winter,
And always the warm, soft smile
of a friend.

Lov'd land of the bards and saints! To me

There's nought so dear as thy minstrelsy;

Bright is Nature's every dress,

Rich in unborrowed loveliness;

Winning is every shape she wears,

Winning is she in thy own sweet airs . . .

Thomas Furlong
Irish poet (1794–1827)

BLESSINGS FROM THE
LAND OF EIRE

There's a dear little plant that
grows in our isle

> 'Twas Saint Patrick himself
> sure that set it

And the sun on his labor with
pleasure did smile

> And a tear from his eyes
> oft-times wet it

It grows through the bog, through
the brake, through the mireland

> And they call it the dear little
> Shamrock of Ireland

Traditional Irish Folk Song

No! no land doth rank
above thee

Or for loveliness or worth

So shall I, from this day forth,

Ever sing and love thee.

James Clarence Mangan
Irish poet (1803–1849)

Blessings from the Land of Eire

May the raindrops fall lightly
on your brow;

May the soft winds freshen
your spirit;

May the sunshine brighten
your heart;

May the burdens of the day
rest lightly upon you;

And may God enfold you in the
mantle of His love.

47

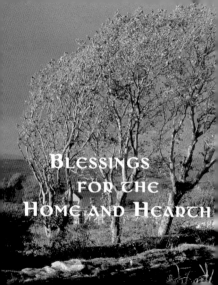

BLESSINGS
FOR THE
HOME AND HEARTH

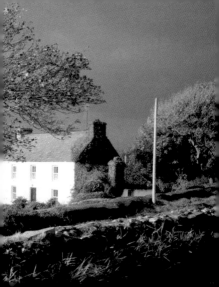

If ever I'm a money'd man,

I mean, please God, to cast
My golden anchor in the place
      where youthful years were
      pass'd

Though heads that bow are
      black and brown must mean-
      while gather grey

New faces rise by every hearth,
      and old ones drop away—

BLESSINGS FOR THE
HOME AND HEARTH

Yet dearer still that Irish hill
    than all the world beside;

It's home, sweet home, where'er
    I roam, through lands and
    waters wide.

And if the Lord allows me,
    I surely will return

To my native Ballyshannon, and
    the winding banks of Erne.

William Allingham
Irish poet (1824–1889)

May your glass
be ever full.

May the roof over your
head be always strong.

And may you be
in heaven half an hour

Before the Devil knows
you're dead.

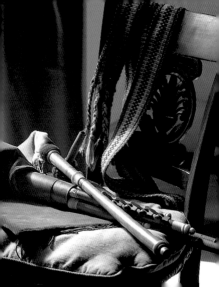

MAY YOU LIVE
AS LONG AS YOU WANT,

AND NEVER WANT
AS LONG AS YOU LIVE.

BLESSINGS FOR THE HOME AND HEARTH

May there always be work for
your hands to do,

May your purse always hold a
coin or two.

May the sun always shine warm
on your windowpane,

May a rainbow be certain to
follow each rain.

May the hand of a friend always
be near you,

And may God fill your heart with
gladness to cheer you.

Health and a long life
to you.

Land without rent to you.

A child every year to you.

And if you can't go
to heaven,

May you at least die in
Ireland.

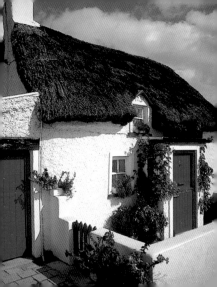

There is not in the wide world a
valley so sweet

As that vale in whose bosom the
bright waters meet;

Oh! the last rays of feeling and
life must depart,

Ere the bloom of that valley shall
fade from my heart.

Thomas Moore
Irish songwriter (1779–1852)

MAY YOU LIVE LONG,

DIE HAPPY,

AND RATE A MANSION
IN HEAVEN.

May your
troubles be less
And your
blessings be more.
And nothing
but happiness
Come through
your door.

May you be poor
in misfortune,

Rich in blessings,

Slow to make enemies,

And quick to make friends.

But rich or poor, quick or slow,

May you know nothing
but happiness

From this day forward.

MAY YOUR RIGHT HAND
ALWAYS
BE STRETCHED OUT
IN FRIENDSHIP
AND NEVER IN WANT.

BLESSINGS FOR THE HOME AND HEARTH

May you have food
and raiment,

A soft pillow for your head;

May you be forty years
in heaven

Before the devil knows
you're dead.

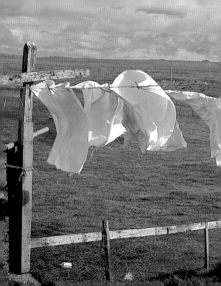

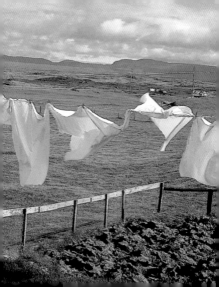

May the roof above us
never fall in,

And may the friends
gathered below it
never fall out.

MAY THERE BE A
GENERATION OF CHILDREN
ON THE CHILDREN OF
YOUR CHILDREN.

O DIM DELICIOUS HEAVEN OF
DREAMS—

    THE LAND OF BOYHOOD'S
       DEWEY GLOW—

AGAIN I HEAR YOUR TORRENT
STREAMS

    THROUGH PURPLE GORGE
      AND VALLEY FLOW,

WHILST FRESH THE MOUNTAIN
BREEZES BLOW.

BLESSINGS FOR THE
HOME AND HEARTH

ABOVE THE AIR SMITES SHARP
AND CLEAR—

    THE SILENT LUCID SPRING
        IT CHILLS

BUT UNDERNEATH, MOVE
WARM AMIDST

    THE BASES OF THE HILLS.

John O'Donnell
Irish poet (1837–1874)

May your neighbors
respect you,

Trouble neglect you,

The angels protect you,

And heaven accept
you.

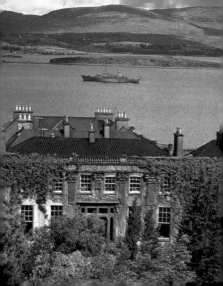

Bless you and yours

As well as the cottage you live in.

May the roof overhead be well
thatched

And those inside be well
matched.

May your troubles be less
And your blessings be more.
And nothing but happiness
Come through your door.

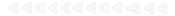

May joy and peace
surround you,

Contentment latch
your door,

And happiness be
with you now

And bless you evermore.

BLESSINGS FOR THE
HOME AND HEARTH

*May your home be filled
with laughter,*

>   *May your pockets be filled
>   with gold,*

*And may you have all the
happiness*

>   *Your Irish heart can hold.*

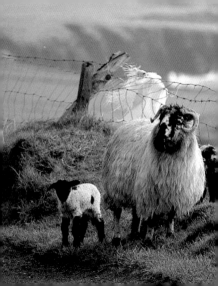

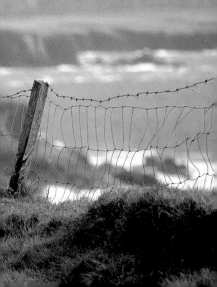

A Blessing for You
and Yours

❀ ❀ ❀

May the grace of God's
protection

And His great love which

Within your home and
within the hearts

Of all who dwell inside.

Walls for the wind

And a roof for the rain,

And drinks by the fire.

Laughter to cheer you

And those you love near you

And all that your heart may
desire!

Bless the four corners of
this house,

    And be the lintel blessed.

Bless the hearth,
    And bless the board,
        And bless each place
            of rest.

And bless the door that opens
to strangers as to kin,

BLESSINGS FOR THE
HOME AND HEARTH

AND BLESS EACH SHINING WINDOW

That lets the sunlight in.

Bless the oak tree overhead,

Bless every sturdy wall,

And may the peace of GOD
above be always on us ALL.

❀ ❀ ❀ ❀ ❀ ❀ ❀ ❀

MAY YOUR
HOME ALWAYS BE TOO
SMALL TO HOLD ALL
OF YOUR FRIENDS.

❀ ❀ ❀ ❀ ❀ ❀ ❀ ❀

82

May those who love us,
love us.

And those who don't love us,

May God turn their hearts.

And if he doesn't
turn their hearts,

May he turn their ankles,

So we may know them
by their limping!

Calm be thy sleep as infants'
slumbers!
Pure as angel thoughts thy
dreams!
May ever joy this bright world
numbers
Shed o'er thee their
mingled beams!

Thomas Moore
Irish songwriter (1779–1852)

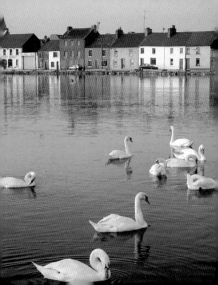

In the December weather,
grey and grim,

In the December twilight,
keen and cold,

Stood the farmhouse on the
green-reached hill

Piled with thatched rooves,
mellowed into gold . . .

John O'Donnell
Irish poet (1837–1874)

St. Brigid's Blessing

✠ ✠ ✠

God bless the poor,
God bless the sick,
God bless our human race;
God bless our food,
God bless our drink
And our homes,
O God, embrace.

St. Brigid of Kildare
6th-century Irish cleric

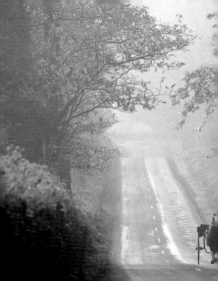

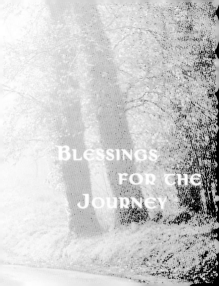

BLESSINGS

FOR THE

JOURNEY

I've wandered by the rolling Lee!
  And Lene's green bowers—
I've seen the Shannon's wide-
    spread sea,
  And Limerick's towers—
And Liffey's tide, where halls of
    pride
  Frown o'er the flood below . . .

Edward Walsh
Irish poet (1805–1850)

May the leprechauns
be near you,

To spread luck
along your way.

And may all the
Irish angels

Smile on you
St. Patrick's Day.

MAY THE BLESSINGS
OF EACH DAY

BE THE BLESSINGS
YOU NEED MOST.

May the road rise to meet
you.
May the wind be always at
your back.
May the sun shine warm upon
your face.
And rains fall soft upon your
fields.
And until we meet again,
May God hold you in the
hollow of His hand.

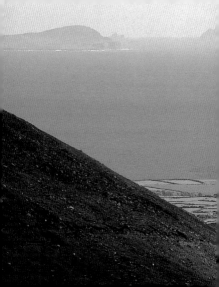

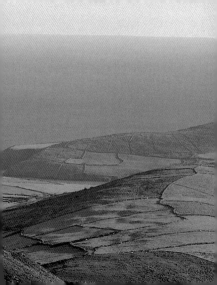

May the blessings of light
be upon you,

Light without and light
within.

And in all your comings
and goings,

May you ever have a
kindly greeting

From them you meet
along the road.

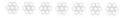

Wherever you go and
whatever you do,

May the luck of the
Irish be there with you.

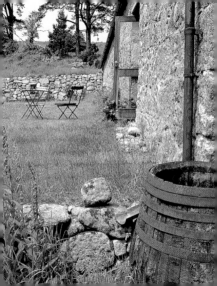

May you have warm words
    on a cold evening,

A full moon on a dark night,

And the road downhill all the
    way to your door.

I will arise and go now,
for always night and day

I hear the lake water lapping
with low sounds by the shore;

While I stand on the roadway,
or on the pavements grey,

I hear it in the deep heart's core.

W.B. Yeats
Irish writer and statesman (1865–1939)

May the good saints
protect you
And bless you today
And may troubles
ignore you
Each step of the way

MAY GOOD LUCK
BE YOUR FRIEND,

IN WHATEVER YOU DO,

AND MAY TROUBLE BE ALWAYS

A STRANGER TO YOU.

Lucky stars above you,
Sunshine on your way,
Many friends to love you,
Joy in work and play,
Laughter to outweigh each care,
In your heart a song,
And gladness waiting everywhere
All your whole life long!

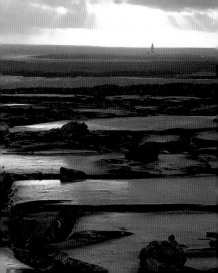

May the lilt of Irish laughter
Lighten every load,
May the mist of Irish magic
Shorten every road,
May you taste the sweetest
    pleasures
That fortune e're bestowed,
And may all your friends
    remember
All the favors you are owed.

She is a rich and rare land,
Oh, she's a fresh and fair land;
She is a dear and rare land,
this native land of mine.

Thomas Davis
Irish poet (1814–1845)

May the love
and protection
Saint Patrick can give
Be yours in abundance
As long as you live.

May you have all the
happiness
And luck that life can hold—
And at the end
of all your rainbows
May you find a pot of gold.

Gaelic Prayer

✠ ✠ ✠

Deep peace of the
running waves to you.
> Deep peace of the
> flowing air to you.
Deep peace of the
smiling stars to you.
> Deep peace of the
> quiet earth to you.
Deep peace of the
watching shepherds to you.
> Deep peace of the
> Son of Peace to you.

109

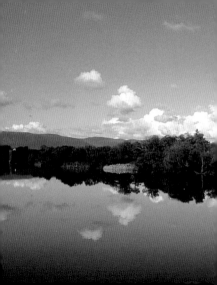

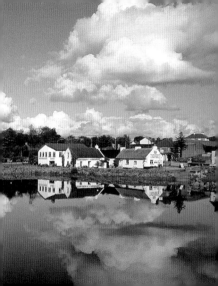

May St. Patrick guard you
wherever

You go and guide you in

Whatever you do—
and may his loving

Protection be a blessing to you
always.

May you have the hindsight to know where you've been,

The foresight to know where you're going,

And the insight to know when you're going too far!

The savage loves his native shore,

> *Though rude the soil and chill the air;*

Well then may Erin's sons adore

> *Their isle, which nature formed so fair!*

What flood reflects a shore so
sweet,

> As Shannon great, or
> past'ral Bann?

Or who a friend or foe can meet,

> As generous as an
> Irishman?

James Orr
Irish poet (1770–1816)

115

IRISH BLESSINGS

May you always have
a clean shirt,
a clean conscience,
and a guinea in your
pocket!

MAY THE LUCK OF THE
IRISH POSSESS YOU;

MAY THE DEVIL FLY OFF
WITH YOUR WORRIES;

MAY GOD BLESS YOU
FOREVER AND EVER.

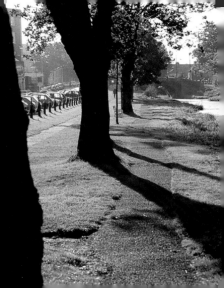

Throughout my journey
    I did not meet

Another country like the land
    of O'Neill;

The variegated hillsides
    bright with dew

The sunny smooth meadows
    crossed by roads.

Pádraigín Haicéad
17th-century Irish poet

It's easy to be pleasant

When life flows by like a
song.

But the man worthwhile is
the one who can smile

When everything goes dead
wrong.

For the test of the heart is
trouble,

And it always comes with
years.

And the smile that is worth
the praises of earth

Is the smile that shines
through the tears.

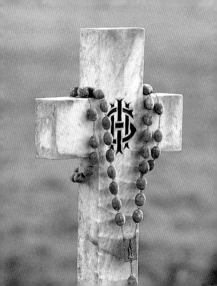

✠ ✠ ✠ ✠ ✠ ✠   ✠

May the Good Lord
take a liking to you,

. . . but not too soon!

✠ ✠ ✠ ✠ ✠ ✠   ✠

*May the saddest day
of your future be no worse
Than the happiest day
of your past.*

ALWAYS REMEMBER TO FORGET

THE TROUBLES THAT PASSED AWAY.

BUT NEVER FORGET TO REMEMBER

THE BLESSINGS THAT

COME EACH DAY.

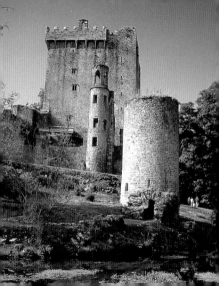

PHOTOGRAPHY CREDITS

This book has been bound
using handcraft methods and Smyth-sewn
to ensure durability.

The dust jacket and interior were
designed by Maria Taffera Lewis.

The text was edited
by Brendan J. Cahill.

Photo research was executed
by Susan Oyama.

The text was set in Comcille and Caslon.